Discard

Careers

People
Who Like
To Perform

Interviews by Russell Shorto

Photographs by Edward Keating and Carrie Boretz

CHOICES
The Millbrook Press
Brookfield, Connecticut

Produced in association with Agincourt Press.

Choices Editor: Megan Liberman

Photographs by Edward Keating, except: Marshall Crenshaw (Carrie
Boretz), Dr. Judy Kuriansky (Carrie Boretz), Stephen A. Kisslinger
(Carrie Boretz), Melinda Lowell (Carrie Boretz), Vince Errico
(Carrie Boretz).

Library of Congress Cataloging-in-Publication Data

Shorto, Russell.
Careers for people who like to perform/interviews by Russell Shorto,
photographs by Edward Keating and Carrie Boretz.

p.   cm. – (Choices)
Includes bibliographical references and index.

Summary: People working in a wide range of performing careers,
including trial lawyer, comedian, dancer, and anchorwoman, describe
the daily routines, benefits, and drawbacks of their jobs and the
education and training they received.

ISBN 1-56294-158-5
ISBN 0-395-63574-8 (pbk.)

1. Vocational guidance – Juvenile literature.
2. Entertainers – United States – Interviews.
3. Professional employees – United States – Interviews.
[1. Vocational guidance.   2. Occupations.   3. Entertainers.]
I. Keating, Edward, ill.   II. Boretz, Carrie, ill.
III. Title.   IV. Series: Choices (Brookfield, Conn.)
HF5381.2.S54   1992   91-27660
790.2′023′73 – dc20

Photographs copyright in the names of the photographers.

Contents

Introduction

In this book, fourteen people who work in performance-related fields talk about their careers – what their work involves, how they got started, and what they like (and dislike) about it. They tell you things you should know before beginning a performance-related career and show you how performance skills can lead to many different types of jobs.

Many of the jobs featured in this book are in the performing arts – such as actor, dancer, comedian, and musician. Others, such as talk show host and news anchorwoman, apply performance skills to work in the broadcast media. Still others – including teacher, pastor, and marketing executive – utilize the ability to perform in much more subtle ways.

The fourteen careers described here are just the beginning, so don't limit your sights. At the end of this book, you'll find short descriptions of a dozen more careers you may want to explore, as well as suggestions on how to get more information. There are many business opportunities for people who enjoy being in front of an audience. If you like to perform, you'll find a wide range of career choices open to you.

Joan E. Storey, M.B.A., M.S.W.
Series Career Consultant

"I happen to like juggling."

FRANK OLIVIER

JUGGLER

Berkeley, California

WHAT I DO:
I'm a juggler and a unicycler, and I say funny things while I'm juggling and unicycling. I juggle balls, clubs, rings, torches, machetes, axes — and I do a routine where I juggle a small child from the audience along with two balls. Right now I'm doing a theater show, which takes up a good amount of my time. I've been working on it for a couple of years.

I have a loose schedule and tend to stay up fairly late at night. Then I sleep as late as I want. I got into that rhythm while I was performing in comedy clubs a few years ago. I wake up in the morning between ten and noon. Then I stretch for half an hour and meditate for half an hour. After that, I eat breakfast and take care of business stuff, return some

phone calls, and practice my juggling. I practice when I want to, not on a set schedule. But I happen to like juggling, so I always practice enough to keep getting better. I might not practice for several days, or I might practice continually for several days.

I have freelance agents who book shows for me, and I also book some shows myself. I perform at comedy clubs, corporate parties, state fairs, benefits, on cruises, and at television shows. I've been on "The Tonight Show," "Comedy Tonight" on PBS, British television, and — believe it or not — "World News Tonight." I even performed once for Princess Margaret as part of a benefit in London.

The theater show I'm doing now brings together dance, big props, unicycles, magic, and juggling. I'm the main person on stage, but I have several other people

Frank juggles clubs while riding a six-foot unicycle.

Frank consults with the stage crew before a show.

working with me. The show is called "Frank Olivier on the Edge," and I've performed it in San Francisco, Berkeley, Portland, and Italy. When they hired me to perform it in Italy, I told them it was in English, but they said, "No trouble." And they were right. Nobody understood English, but they treated me very well. They got the physical stuff.

HOW I GOT STARTED:
I started juggling when I was 9. A fireman came to our third-grade class and taught fire safety using juggling. I was entranced. I worked at juggling on my own for about a year, trying to learn to juggle three balls in a circle, which is very difficult. Then somebody showed me an easier way, throwing the balls up the middle. I caught on right away.

I practiced on my own until I graduated from high school. Then I went to the Ringling Brothers Clown College, which is eight weeks long. When I finished, I turned down a contract with the circus because I didn't want to be a clown. Instead, I started doing street performing in San Francisco. I did that for four years, and in the meantime I started getting into comedy clubs. As time went on, it got easier and easier to get work. Then I went to New York, and I landed a role in *Sugar Babies*, an old burlesque-style musical, starring Mickey Rooney. That was pretty amazing. It doesn't happen that way for most people.

HOW I FEEL ABOUT IT:
I think that you lead a charmed life by doing what you want and not worrying too much. Right now I live in an old antique shop. It's a huge space with high ceilings, so I can practice easily, and it's got lots of light.

I love doing what I do. I wouldn't trade it for anything. I've been very fortunate to be able to do something I enjoy so much. I can imagine that some people might not enjoy being a juggler, but for me it's ideal. You don't always know when money is coming in. And you go through slow times when people aren't hiring jugglers. Sometimes, I even get tired of it. But that feeling never lasts long.

WHAT YOU SHOULD KNOW:
It's very useful to find out where jugglers meet so that you can be around them. In most big cities, there are set meeting places. In San Francisco, for instance, jugglers meet on Saturday afternoons in Golden Gate Park. You can

also learn juggling from books, but that's not as good as learning from a teacher. Learning from an expert is better than figuring it out for yourself.

The money depends on how hard you want to work. You can make about $30,000 to $40,000 a year if you're a good juggler and you work at it. Most bookings pay about $1,500 a week.

Frank performs a challenging five-club comedic juggle.

"It's a real thrill to see your picture in a magazine."

AMY ELMORE

MODEL

New York, New York

WHAT I DO:
I travel all over the world to pose for magazines, catalogs, fashion shows, and television commercials. I'm self-employed, but I have agents who work to promote me in the fashion industry. I've been in the business for two and a half years now.

There is no such thing as a typical day for me. One day, I might get up at five in the morning for a shoot. The next day, if I don't have anything scheduled, I might go on a casting call, which is an audition for a job.

Posing for a shoot is a lot like acting. You can't just stand there and smile at the camera. You have to communicate something. Sometimes I pose for hundreds of pictures just to get one that's right.

I also spend a lot of my time traveling to different

Amy poses during a fashion shoot for a department store catalog.

jobs. I've been to Japan, Australia, Africa, and all over Europe and the Caribbean. Models travel for different reasons. Sometimes it's to work for a foreign magazine. For instance, I do a lot of work for European magazines, which involves traveling to France and Italy. Also, clients occasionally want specific backgrounds for their photos. If a client wants a safari background, for example, then I might travel to Africa.

HOW I GOT STARTED:
When I was in high school, I entered and won a modeling contest sponsored by *Seventeen* magazine, and that's how I got my start. My first professional modeling job was in Japan. I had never been away from my family before, so it was a little scary. But Japan is a great place to have your first foreign assignment because it's such a safe country.

A stylist works on Amy's hair between photographic sessions.

After that first job, I did a lot of work in Europe. Models often work in Europe before they do much modeling in America. There are so many fashion magazines in Europe that it's often easier to get started there.

HOW I FEEL ABOUT IT: Modeling can be a very exciting business. Traveling is my favorite part of the job. It has brought me close friends all over the world. For instance, one of my best friends is Dutch, and I would never have met her if I hadn't been in this business. It's also a real thrill to see your picture in a magazine. It makes all the hard work worthwhile.

But it's not fun and glamour all the time. You have to be a very strong person to survive in this business because there are many ups and downs. For every job you get, there are a lot you lose. You have to keep pushing for the jobs you want, but you can't take it personally when you're turned down. It takes time to get noticed, and you have to be willing to stand the rejections until you are.

You also have to be somewhat of an extrovert to do this. You have to like getting up in front of a camera and a large group of people and performing for them. If you can't handle public attention, you'll never make it as a model.

There are also more specific drawbacks to being in the public eye. You're on display so much of the time that when you're not working, you want to be left alone. But that's not always possible. Someone may stop you in the street because they've seen your face or read an article about you, which can be a hassle. But that's the price you pay for this kind of work.

WHAT YOU SHOULD KNOW:
There are a lot of things to know if you want to go into this business. For one, if you're a woman, you have to be at least five-foot nine. And you have to keep your weight down. You also need to have a head for business.

The money in modeling varies incredibly. Some people only pay their bills the first year, while others make a lot of money right away. It's really hard to say. It often depends on the kind of work you want do. If you just want to make money, you can model for catalogs and make $800 to $5,000 a day. But if you want more prestigious work, then you model for magazines, though they don't pay nearly as well.

The pay scale for commercials is high. In Europe, a commercial will pay around $10,000. In America, a national commercial might pay $30,000. Of course, if you really hit it big in this business, you'll make millions. But there are very few people who make it to the top.

During a shoot, Amy is the focus of everyone's attention.

"You aren't taught how to play rock and roll."

MARSHALL CRENSHAW

MUSICIAN

Woodstock, New York

WHAT I DO:

I'm a songwriter, a guitarist, and a singer. I make records, and I also perform on stage. I make a record about once every two years, and there's a kind of routine to it. Writing the songs usually takes twelve to fifteen months. Then recording them takes another two to three months in the studio.

Once the recording is done, I usually go out on tour to perform the new songs and support the record. A tour might last anywhere from three to six months. Then I start working on the next record. All the time, however, I'm working on my performing skills: my guitar playing and my singing. You aren't taught how to play rock and roll music. You learn it by listening to others and then doing it yourself.

Marshall sings one of his hits at a concert in New York City.

I've been making records for about ten years now. For the first three or four years, I had a band, but there tends to be a lot of wear and tear on the egos in a band. That's why groups usually don't stay together. Also, I like the flexibility of working on my own and picking and choosing my collaborators. It keeps things fresh.

HOW I GOT STARTED:

I come from a musical family. My father was a rock and roll fan, and I heard the music around the house while I was growing up. I was naturally drawn to it. I took piano lessons when I was nine and started playing the guitar when I was ten. I was in rock bands all during high school.

After high school, I spent three or four years working in a succession of factory jobs. I worked in a snow-mobile factory for a while.

Marshall tunes up while stagehands adjust the lighting.

Then, when I was 23, I started playing in bar bands as a full-time rock musician. I was part-owner of a recording studio for a while, which gave me an opportunity to sharpen my skills as a recording artist. Finally, in 1981, I moved from the Detroit area to New York City and started making my own records.

HOW I FEEL ABOUT IT:
I am totally absorbed by what I do, because this work gives me a chance to see the world from a unique perspective. Also, it gives me a lot of control over my time and the direction of my life.

The marketplace moves at a very fast pace, however, because this business really thrives on novelty. What's good is that it prods you to keep developing and using your imagination. You have to be open to new things in order to survive.

On the negative side, it's very, very competitive. Also, it's a very tough business. There are a lot of shady characters, and when you first learn about them – if you come from a sheltered background – it's very shocking.

Other drawbacks are harder to define. If you have a bad show, for example, or you find that you're not connecting with the audience, that can be very frustrating. Or if you have a record that's not as successful as your previous one, it tends to put you in a spiritual quandary. You start wondering what you did wrong, or whether you did anything wrong.

The best times for me are when I can just sit down and do the work for my own enjoyment. I find that the stuff I've had the most success with is the stuff that was done while I was in this pure state. Some musicians can manufacture for the marketplace, but I don't enjoy doing that.

WHAT YOU SHOULD KNOW:
You have to love this work because there are a lot of hardships you'll have to endure. You have to go into it for the love of the music, out of an undeniable urge to express yourself and communicate with people. Also, don't try to second-guess your audience. Respect them. Work hard, and give it everything you've got. If you're ambivalent about your work, you'll never succeed.

Of course, you can make a fortune playing rock and roll music. But not everyone does. In fact, hardly anyone does. There's no such thing as a quick buck. You have to be lucky, and you have to be smart. It's a business.

Marshall reads a review of his album in a music paper.

"All my life, all day long, I'm joking around."

WALLI COLLINS

COMEDIAN

Springfield, Massachusetts

WHAT I DO:
I'm a professional comedian. I stand up in front of people and tell them funny stories. That's it.

Just kidding. During the day, I'm either arranging gigs or trying to get my travel plans together. I perform at colleges all over the country, so I try to line up several colleges when I know I'm going to be in a particular area. For example, I might get a gig in Gary, Indiana, and then use that as a base for dates in other parts of the state.

When I'm on the road, I drive around a lot. When I arrive at a college, I familiarize myself with the school, talk to some of the students, and check out the town. Then I get something to eat, take a nap, and get ready for the show.

Walli performs one of his many stand-up routines at a comedy nightclub.

My routine is different when I'm performing at a nightclub. Nightclub gigs are usually for more than one night — generally, Wednesday through Saturday. I might do one show a day on Wednesday and Thursday, two shows on Friday, and three on Saturday. Sometimes I even do one on Sunday.

To prepare for a show, I run through my material book to refresh myself. Sometimes, I also practice my new stuff to make sure I get it right. Beyond that, all my life, all day, I'm joking around. And that's preparation, too. I don't suddenly transform myself into "Jokeman" for the stage.

HOW I GOT STARTED:
After college, I went to architecture school and got work as an architect for a while. Then one day while I was talking to my mother, she asked me what I would

Walli meets with the stage manager before a show.

do if I could do anything.
I said I'd like to be an actor.
Then she asked me why I was
an architect. She said I'd
never know how good an
actor I could be unless I tried.

I thought I'd try comedy
first because I could control
the pace and the material. So
I went to a comedy club and
auditioned. I stunk the place
up. It was terrible. I decided
right then and there that
I wasn't right for it. But the
emcee of the show stopped
me as I was leaving. He said
I shouldn't give up because
I have "the gift," meaning
stage presence. If you have it,
people are relaxed and enjoy
your company on stage. It's
God-given, not something
you can learn.

The emcee gave me five
dollars and told me to come
back the next week. I couldn't
believe it. I kept going back
for a year. In that time,
I learned my shtick, which is
the collection of mannerisms
and attitudes that makes
each comedian different. My
shtick is being clean — not
swearing, no racial jokes.
Instead, I talk about my child-
hood, my parents — things
everybody can relate to.
I started professionally in
1984, and I've been at it
ever since.

HOW I FEEL ABOUT IT:
I love my work. It's a fantasy
that I had and pursued. I fol-
lowed my dream, and it came
true. I'm able to support
myself, I enjoy going to work,
and I look forward to the
next day. There are a few
problems, however. I have a
nine-year-old daughter, and
because I travel a lot I'm not
able to hang out with her as
much as I'd like.

WHAT YOU SHOULD KNOW:
What I've learned is that the thing you feel is right for you is usually the thing you should pursue. We're on this earth for a reason. We all have a gift. Take that gift and use it. There are no limits to what you can do, but you'll never know unless you go out and give it a try.

Keep in mind, however, that everything takes time. You really have to learn patience. Also, don't feel that there may be only one single thing that's right for you. You probably have related strengths. Try them all. I thought I was going to be an actor. Now I'm a comedian. But I'm still taking acting lessons, and I'm writing a pilot episode for a television situation comedy.

The money in comedy can be good. Don't expect to make a million dollars your first year, but after two years ... no, I'm just kidding again. You start out at maybe $15 or $20 for a twenty-minute set at a showcase club. That isn't great, but the showcase rooms in big cities are important because agents frequent them. Robin Williams, Michael Keaton, and Bill Cosby were all doing stand-up in showcase rooms when they were discovered. For college shows, you can make from $500 on up. In comedy clubs, you can make anything from $50 for emceeing to $200 or more for headlining the show.

Walli laughs with the audience at one of his jokes.

"I didn't plan on doing this when I was growing up."

DR. JUDY KURIANSKY

TALK SHOW HOST

New York, New York

WHAT I DO:

I'm a call-in radio host who gives advice on the air. I started in 1980, when call-in advice shows were just starting to become popular. I do a three-hour show five nights a week as well as some other radio work, such as filling in on WABC Talk Radio.

Besides taking calls from listeners, I also invite celebrities onto my show to talk about their problems. I have had Lucy Arnaz talking about her family, Keith Hernandez talking about how to win in sports, and Siskel and Ebert talking about sibling rivalry. I also do some television work. I used to be a reporter for WABC-TV, WPIX-TV, and several other stations. Now I do reports for the CNBC cable network and appear live to discuss the news.

Judy hosts a three-hour radio program five nights a week.

HOW I GOT STARTED:

I didn't plan on doing this when I was growing up. My father told me to go into computers, so I studied trigonometry and was a math major in college. Then I got into psychology and realized that I cared more about people than I did about numbers.

After I began working as a psychologist, I did a research study involving the advertising of over-the-counter drugs on television. It became a news story, and I was asked to go on television shows to talk about it. I was a good guest, and they kept inviting me back.

One time I was asked to be a guest on a morning show that was testing new hosts. The program director told me I was better than the hosts he was testing, and he asked me to become a regular.

Later, the general manager of a radio station asked me to be the host of a call-in

Judy takes another phone call from a listener.

advice show he was planning. I like to take on new challenges, so I agreed to do it.

HOW I FEEL ABOUT IT:
As my friends who are astrologists say, this job fits my chart perfectly. Broadcasting is on the cutting edge of what's happening today. When I appear on radio shows around the country, I get a sense of what people are talking about nationwide, and this allows me to stay in touch with public opinion. One thing I've learned is that there are many more similarities among people around the country than one might think. People want to feel they're connected to each other. They want to know they're not the only ones who feel the way they do.

Radio is also a very exciting medium. It allows me to interact with the audience, which in turn creates tremendous energy. There are times when I do overnight call-in shows from midnight until 6:00 A.M., but I never get tired because there's always such an exciting interchange with the callers. Every time a person calls, it's like opening a Christmas present. And when a show's over, I feel more alive, not more tired.

WHAT YOU SHOULD KNOW:
Radio is right only for a certain type of person. You have to love people, and you

have to love the exchange of ideas. I was trained as a psychologist in the Freudian method, according to which the doctor just sits there and listens. But I learned quickly that the Freudian approach doesn't work in this business. Instead, you have to perform, and you have to tell an interesting story.

There are many ways to get into this business, but I recommend becoming an intern. That way, you get to meet people in the business and make yourself valuable to them. Today, kids demand so much right away that they cut their own throats. It's better to have a more cooperative temperament. Be willing to help the person you work for. In television particularly, you don't say no. You find a way to get around problems. You make it work. Always pitch in and do your best.

The money varies quite a lot, depending on whether you work for a small local station, a big-city station, or a network. A production assistant in radio may earn $8 an hour, or about $17,000 to $25,000 a year, while hosts can make $25,000 to $50,000 in smaller markets. Pay also depends on the time and day of the week you're on. People who host morning shows in big markets can make several hundred thousand dollars a year.

Judy sometimes does overnight radio call-in shows.

"I play mostly bad guys and cops."

CARL CIARFALIO

STUNTMAN

North Hollywood, California

WHAT I DO:

I work as both a stuntman and an actor in television shows, movies, and commercials. I play mostly bad guys and cops. I've been in *Commando*, *Beetlejuice*, *Licence to Kill*, *Out for Justice*, *Robocop 2*, and *Against All Odds*. Sometimes, actors will request me as their stunt double. I've doubled for Alex Karras and Lou Ferrigno.

Stunt work is very much freelance. I'm hired by a stunt coordinator, who has been hired by a production company to manage the stunts for a particular movie. The stunt coordinator goes through the script and says, "We need four cops, three heavies, a goon, and a double for the actor." Then he looks for people who fit those parts. The bad guy roles are called goons, thugs, heavies,

Carl uses his athletic ability to accomplish difficult stunts.

and mad dogs. These characters sit in the background and maybe have two or three lines.

It's important to get to know the good stunt coordinators. Because they're constantly making movies, you get a lot of calls. Also, even though the work is freelance, there are still some influential organizations within the stunt business. We have three prominent men's groups and two women's groups, which you have to be asked to join. I'm a member of the Stuntman's Association, which provides a home base and a brotherhood for me. It's nice to have that sort of thing behind you in this business.

HOW I GOT STARTED:

I was an athlete in high school and college, playing football and doing judo and other sports. One summer, a friend who had done some

Carl plays a mad dog in this Hollywood feature film.

stunt work told me about an audition for stuntmen. He taught me how to fake a fight and a little about what the coordinators were looking for. The physical stuff came very easily to me, and the character stuff came, too, because I'm theatrical. The audition went well, and I got a job for the summer.

I did a lot of different things in the beginning. I was in some student films. I did my first real movie in 1977, and I stayed with it. I kept learning and meeting people all the time.

HOW I FEEL ABOUT IT:
Through sports, I got used to being a team player, which is important in my line of work. As a stuntman, you're a member of a team. You know that if you're on fire, other people have to put you out. You have to trust them, and they have to trust you. When you do develop that trust, it's a great feeling.

Then there's the satisfaction of the work itself. My acting has come a long way. I just finished an episode of "The Flash," for instance, in which my part included not only stunts but dialogue as well.

The downside is the chance of injury. You need to know when to say no to a physical challenge — when it's just too much. And I have said no to certain stunts.

WHAT YOU SHOULD KNOW: There are many different paths to stunt work, but they all share one thing: You have to knock on doors, and you have to be assertive without being aggressive. The more you have to offer, the better your chances are. I learned acting, and by offering that, I became more valuable. I also think college is a wonderful thing that shouldn't be passed up. It gives you not only a degree, but also life experience that's invaluable.

If you want to do this work, you need to be in California, New York, Florida, or Atlanta — places where a lot of films are shot. You have to go to the set where they're shooting and do whatever you can to get yourself noticed. I used to sneak onto sets with pictures of myself and a resume.

As for the pay, the base salary is $431 a day. You might stand around all day, throw one punch, and leave with your $431. But you get paid more for stunts. If you perform a stunt such as getting hit by a car, it might boost your pay up to $3,000 for the day. Every show has a different budget, which translates into different prices for different stunts. A fall might pay $1,000 in one show and $200 in another. In terms of a yearly salary, you could make anywhere from $30,000 to $300,000.

Carl puts on protective gear for a motorcycle stunt.

"I've gotten to play crazy people, doctors, lawyers, businessmen, and tramps."

JOHN TILLOTSON

ACTOR

New York, New York

WHAT I DO:
I work primarily professional regional theaters throughout the United States. But I've done just about everything an actor can do: commercials, television dramas, soap operas, industrial films, and even one movie. I'm what's called a character actor, which means that I can play a wide variety of roles. I've gotten to play crazy people, school teachers, doctors, lawyers, clergymen, businessmen, and tramps.

I work all over the country. Right now I'm doing a play in Delaware, where I'm in residence for six weeks. Because it's so close to New York, I go home frequently. At other times, however, I might be in residence for nine months and rarely go home at all.

John plays the role of a hobo in a musical comedy staged at a regional resident theater.

The way I got my current role is fairly typical of the process. I have an agent, who submitted my publicity photo and resume to a casting director. The casting director then arranged for me to audition with the producer and director of the play. I went to the first audition and did well enough to be called back. The call-back usually involves reading lines from the play itself. Two days later, my agent called to say they wanted me for the play.

I waited three weeks for the rehearsals to begin, then we had three and a half weeks of full-time rehearsals, working eight hours a day, six days a week. During the rehearsals, you learn your lines and find out how you're going to move on stage. You also learn what the play's about and how best to play your role.

After rehearsals come the preview performances, dur-

HOW I GOT STARTED:

I always wanted to be an actor. When I was a kid, my parents had the original Broadway cast recording of *My Fair Lady*, and I remember listening to it and thinking about performing it myself.

In kindergarten, I was in a play and liked it. Then, in the first or second grade, I played Santa Claus in *The Night Before Christmas*. I was also involved in magic shows and marionette plays. Being a performer has always been a strong impulse of mine. I went to Southern Methodist University, where I majored in theater. Then I moved to New York City and started doing showcases to get agents interested in me. A showcase is a full production of a play, but you don't get paid. You do it to be seen. Soon, I started meeting people and got an agent.

HOW I FEEL ABOUT IT:

I like acting a lot. On the other hand, I've thought about getting out of it because it's a hard life. You go through emotional ups and downs. And you're out of work a lot. Last year, I was employed for nine months in four plays and also made some commercials, so I did well financially. But this year I've been in only one play.

Then there's the art of acting, which is basically

John rehearses his lines for a commercial shoot scheduled later in the day.

ing which you get a chance to try the play out in front of a real audience. Then there's opening night, when the critics come so they can write their reviews. The run of a play varies in resident theaters, but it's usually from two to eight weeks.

creating illusions of other people's lives. If you're going to play a truck driver, you have to find out what that life is all about. You have to observe it and then transform yourself into that other person. It's part of the joy in being an actor for me.

WHAT YOU SHOULD KNOW:
Don't do this. That's my first advice to everybody. If you can do anything else and be happy with it, do that other thing. But if you can't — if you must go into acting — be completely committed. If you can't be committed, I don't want to work with you onstage, and neither does any other actor.

I heartily recommend going to acting school. Yale and Julliard have the best visibility. Graduates of those programs seem to have the best shots at jobs. However, there are many smaller programs with equal, if not better, training. Some people come to acting from other fields, but training in the art of acting is very important.

A regional theater job might pay from $375 to $800 a week. On Broadway, the minimum is about $900 a week. A typical actor's salary — working regional theaters and doing some commercials — might be $20,000 to $30,000 a year, if you're very lucky.

John looks through a trade paper for casting calls.

"There's no typical day for me because everything depends on the news."

RENEE POUSSAINT
NEWS ANCHORWOMAN
Washington, D.C.

WHAT I DO:
My primary responsibility is to co-anchor the 5:30 P.M. and 11:00 P.M. newscasts on WJLA-TV, the ABC affiliate in Washington, D.C. But I also do special assignment reporting if there's a major story. Beyond that, I do regular newsmaker profiles of people in the news as well as a lot of community work — making speeches at community meetings and appearing at schools.

It's difficult to describe a typical day for me because everything depends on the news. When there's a major story, such as the war in the Persian Gulf, my day might start with an interview of someone involved. That might happen at around 10:00 A.M. After the interview, I'll listen to the playback, write my report,

Renee breaks for a commercial during her nightly newscast.

and go down to the editing department to discuss the piece with the tape editor. Together, we look over what the cameraman has shot and decide whether my report works well with the pictures. If it does, we'll record what I've written. If there's a problem, I may change the copy to make the piece work better.

When we're done, I'll go back to my office and sort through my mail. Then I'll start looking at the rundown of the newscast, which is a list the producer puts together of the stories for the half-hour show. I'll talk to the producer about each one and look over whatever copy has been written. Normally, I'll rewrite the copy so that it conforms more closely to the way I speak.

Finally, after a last discussion with the producer, I put on my makeup, get my copy together, and head for the set. In between shows, I'll

Renee conducts an interview during the newscast.

normally break for a meal. Sometimes, I'll even be the emcee at a fund-raising dinner or make a speech. Then I come back to the studio and repeat the process for the 11:00 P.M. newscast.

HOW I GOT STARTED:

I started my journalism career in the Columbia University Michelle Clark Fellowship Program for Minority Journalists. After college, I went to work at WBBM-TV in Chicago as a junior writer and then a junior reporter. A year and a half later, I was offered the chance to become a network correspondent, and I joined CBS News' Midwest bureau. Then I spent some time living on the road before trans-ferring to the Washington, D.C., bureau. I remained with CBS network news until 1977, when I was offered the chance to become a local anchor here in D.C. for WJLA-TV.

HOW I FEEL ABOUT IT:

This is one of the most interesting jobs that anyone could have. But as a news anchor, you're a public figure, and that takes some getting used to. There's a certain loss of privacy, and whether you like it or not, you become a role model. When you go out to a restaurant or take your clothes to the cleaners, people come up to you. Most of the time they have something pleasant to say, but sometimes they can be upset about a story you've reported.

You have to be understanding and open.

The downside is the stress. You work with a lot of very tight deadlines, so you have to be able to work well under pressure. You also have to be very flexible because this is a business that depends on technology, and technology can fail.

WHAT YOU SHOULD KNOW:
The main thing is to get as well-rounded an education as you possibly can. A broadcast reporter is often thrown into situations with no background information at all. You're expected to know enough about a subject to figure out what questions to ask. Most important of all, however, it's necessary to have a good education so that you can read and write well. It's your job to understand and translate information for the viewer.

I would also suggest that you work for your school newspaper or college radio station. Or you might volunteer to work at a local television station. Hands-on experience is extremely important. Not only can you learn skills, but you can also learn whether you're comfortable doing the kinds of things that reporters do.

A common misconception is that everyone in television makes a lot of money. If you work at a small-town station the salary can be quite low — in the $20,000 range. On the other end of the spectrum, anchors for a national network can make in the millions. But there are only a handful of people in that range. The vast majority make much less than that.

Renee reviews her copy as she prepares for a broadcast.

"I get excited every time I see the Capitol dome."

JIM McDERMOTT

CONGRESSMAN

Seattle, Washington

WHAT I DO:
I have an extremely challenging job: representing nearly half a million people from the Seattle area in the U.S. Congress. It's my responsibility to figure out what my constituents want done and then to make those things happen.

For example, if my constituents want a better health care system — which they do — I work toward developing a national health care plan. There is also a lot of interest in the environment in my district. Specifically, my constituents want me to save the old-growth forests of Washington state. It helps that I sit on the Interior Committee, which works on laws to safeguard the environment and protect our ancient forests.

Jim is particularly active when it comes to legislation affecting health care issues.

I spend about two thirds of my time in Washington, D.C. There, I'm involved in passing laws and meeting with constituents who have problems they think I can help them with. Sometimes, I work with other congressmen on matters of joint interest. For example, there are old-growth forests in Oregon and northern California as well as in Washington, so I often get together with representatives from those areas to discuss how we'll convince the rest of the Congress to save these forests.

When I'm back home in Seattle, I go to meetings, speak at schools, and do television and radio spots. This is the performance side of the job. Some parts of it are fun, such as being in a parade. Others can be difficult, such as giving a speech to people who aren't crazy about the way you represent them.

Jim has to direct a very large and active staff.

Another big part of what I do is run for reelection, which means meeting people and convincing them that you're the best person to represent them. You've got to be comfortable standing in front of people, putting yourself and your ideas before them. The campaign proper is only three months long, but in a sense you're always campaigning. Over the course of a two-year term, you probably spend 10 to 15 percent of your time running for reelection.

HOW I GOT STARTED:
My path has been very unusual. Initially, I was trained as a physician — a child psychiatrist. But then I served in the navy during the Vietnam War, and it changed my thinking. I knew that I could easily spend the rest of my life in an office, dealing with people one at a time. But I believed that I could have more impact working to pass laws, because laws affect everyone.

I ran for the state legislature and won, so I spent the next fifteen years as a part-time physician and part-time legislator. Then, in 1987, I quit politics, returned to being a full-time physician, and took a job with the State Department in Africa. But things didn't turn out to be that simple. I got a call from some friends who told me about an open congressional seat. Having been interested in national health insurance,

I saw the open seat as an opportunity to work for health care reform. So I ran for Congress in 1988 and won with 77 percent of the vote.

HOW I FEEL ABOUT IT:

Former Speaker of the House John McCormack once said that if you can see the Capitol dome every morning and not get excited, then you've either been here too long or you should never have come in the first place. I get excited every time I see it.

I think it's a high honor to represent your fellow citizens. Much of the work may sound dry and boring, but the excitement lies in trying to make the country a better place to live. It's unfortunate public service has fallen into such disrepute that today few young people think of it as a career. It's the most exciting job I can imagine.

WHAT YOU SHOULD KNOW:

There are many ways to get started in politics. One is to work as a campaign volunteer. Another is to work for a congressman, either in a district office or in Washington, D.C. We don't pay much, but the kids who work for me really get a feeling for what politics is all about.

It's impossible to generalize about what kind of person you should be.

Sometimes I look around the Congress and think, "How did that person get elected?" But other people probably think the same about me. Persistence is the key. If you believe in something, and you work hard enough at it, you can make a change.

You're not going to make as much money in public service as you would in the private sector. The trade-off is that you have the opportunity to change the world in which you live. I've probably given up $450,000 in income over the last fifteen years, but I don't regret it.

Jim goes over his schedule with a legislative aide.

"I try to shape a message that will be convincing, meaningful, and appealing."

STEPHEN A. KISSLINGER

PASTOR

Bentleyville, Pennsylvania

WHAT I DO:
I'm an ordained minister. What I do is try to understand and communicate the Gospel of Jesus Christ. There are four principle goals associated with my ministry: to be a lifelong student of the Gospel, to preach and teach from the Gospel, to care for people, and to be a leader in the Church.

There is also a wide variety of secondary tasks that ministers might take on, depending on the community in which their church is located. I'm a solo pastor in a relatively small town, which means that I work alone. I preach just about every week, and I'm the main leader of the youth group. I also teach classes occasionally, including a premarital class and a confirmation class, which is for people who want to join the church. And I visit people who are elderly and shut-in, or who are facing some specific crisis. I make about twenty to thirty of these visits a month.

Preparing for worship, however, is at the center of what I do — though it's also true that much of what I do during the week works its way into my sermons. Delivering sermons gives me a chance to bring the word of God into people's lives. It's both a great responsibility and a privilege.

The first step in preparing a sermon is researching and understanding the Bible portion for that week. The second involves relating my understanding of the Bible to the needs of the people in my area. There has to be a matching of the meaning of the Bible and the needs of the people. This is the function of the sermon. I try to

Stephen delivers a sermon during a worship service.

find a way to shape a message that will be convincing, meaningful, and appealing, so that people will find renewal and guidance in the words that they hear.

Although there are differences between sermons and other types of performance, there are also some similarities. One is stage fright. It's just you up there all alone in the spotlight. You can't help being aware that people are watching and judging you. I want to come out and be the best communicator I can be — convincing, truthful, exciting, and meaningful. But I know that it is never just my work, that God is working with me in this process.

HOW I GOT STARTED:

I didn't decide to enter a seminary until after I graduated from college. While I was an undergraduate, I thought I would become a lawyer because I wanted to interact with people and help them. As I grew more involved with the Church, however, I became convinced that I could be most effective putting my faith to practical use in the ministry.

I spent four years at a seminary: three years in class work and one as an intern in a church, where I basically did the work of a minister but without the credentials. That was in addition to four years of college.

HOW I FEEL ABOUT IT:

I find my work exciting, challenging, and extremely meaningful. I see the results of my efforts every day in both small and large changes

Stephen talks with a member of his congregation.

Stephen relaxes in the park with two church members.

in people's lives. It's also a continual learning experience for me. I feel that I am indeed a lifelong student, both of the Bible and of human nature.

The downside of being a solo pastor is the very heavy demand on my time and energy. Sometimes I feel as though there is not enough of me to go around.

The other main problem is that there is not much privacy. It's hard to escape from the role of being a minister. Many people are not willing to allow me to be my own person. They have very high expectations, some of which are not realistic.

WHAT YOU SHOULD KNOW:
There are some ministers who are shy, but you really should like being with people. A concern for others and a willingness to put your own needs on hold are also important. And you have to have a strong personal faith.

If you are looking to get rich, this is the wrong field, but that's not to say the pay is trifling. If you belong to a major denomination, you can be comfortable in the ministry. The pay is roughly comparable to that of a public school teacher. There are a few ministers at prestigious churches in large cities who make $100,000 or more, but they are far from the norm.

"Being persuasive is the key to winning a trial."

MELINDA LOWELL

TRIAL LAWYER

Fort Lee, New Jersey

WHAT I DO:
I have my own law firm and three attorneys working for me. I do a lot of trial work, from matrimonial to personal injury cases, as well as corporate litigation. But matrimonial law is my specialty.

First thing in the morning, I'm usually at the courthouse where I deal with three to five cases at different stages of litigation. I might be filing a motion for temporary support for a wife and children. Or I might be scheduled for an oral argument in front of a judge, with the opposing attorney arguing the other side. Another case might involve the custody of children whose parents are separating. And still another might involve someone indicted for drug possession.

During a break in a trial, Melinda reviews her notes on the courthouse steps.

Later in the morning, I might meet with other lawyers to try and settle a case out of court. Often, these conferences take place before a panel of impartial attorneys who are there to help both sides reach a settlement. Periodically, you go out into the hallway and consult with your client. Then, you go back in again and resume the discussion with the opposing attorneys. You go back and forth until you're able to settle.

I usually get back to my office around 1:30 P.M., and for the rest of the afternoon, I'll meet with clients and prepare for upcoming trials. This might involve legal research, reviewing strategies, or deciding which witnesses should be questioned and how.

Preparing for court is the most important part of my job. The lawyer who is better prepared is usually the one who wins, so I'm always getting ready for trial — rehearsing my case, going over my opening and closing arguments, and making sure there's nothing I've forgotten. It's a twenty-four-hour-a-day commitment. Sometimes, I even get up in the middle of the night and dictate into my answering machine.

HOW I GOT STARTED:

During my first year in college, I had a constitutional law professor who was very inspirational. And while I was still in college, I worked for the Senate Watergate Committee, which convinced me that I wanted to be a lawyer. I went to law school and afterward worked for a prosecutor's office, trying cases and working right in the courthouse. Later, I left to work for a small Park Avenue law firm, which trained me in civil litigation. Eventually I opened my own practice.

HOW I FEEL ABOUT IT:

My work is very exciting. Each case is different, and you're always looking at things from a new perspective. Whichever side you're on, though, trial work requires a great desire to win.

But it can also be draining. A trial means two people can't agree on how to resolve a dispute, so you're fighting all the time. It's a battle, which makes it a difficult chore day in and day out. You have to have a lot of stamina.

Also, it's theater. Depending on the judge and your adversary, you can play a case many different ways. If I have a male chauvinist judge, I

Melinda tries to settle a case out of court.

Melinda files a brief at the county courthouse.

play it very low key. Older senior judges tend to look at me as a daughter, so I play that role, too. You also have to play your adversary. It's a three-ring circus. And even though these performance factors have nothing to do with the facts of the case, you have to take them into consideration.

WHAT YOU SHOULD KNOW:

To be a trial lawyer, you have to be able to get along with people, to read them, and to know when to open your mouth and when to shut it. You also have to be quick on your feet so that you can respond effectively to a judge's questions, or comments made by your adversary.

Intellectually, you need an analytical mind as well as the ability to strategize. If you're good with numbers but find accounting boring, go into law. Numbers come into play in every aspect of the legal profession, so any lawyer who's good at math will excel.

In support of all this, you need to be organized and articulate so that you can present your case in a clear and coherent manner. Being persuasive is the key to winning a trial.

You can make anywhere from $25,000 to $90,000 a year starting out, and you can always earn a good living. If you go into real estate law or commercial practice, the economy can affect you. But if you're in litigation, changes in the economy don't affect you as severely.

"When I teach,
I perform."

ANITA D'ANGELO

DANCER

Miami, Florida

WHAT I DO:

Most of my life has been devoted to dance. Right now, I teach dance at a spa. I also teach aerobics. Dancers tend to snub aerobics, but I span the gap.

I've been teaching here for nine months. Before that, I was pursuing a career as a dancer and actress in New York. At some point, I'll go back to performing, but for now I'm on hiatus from the stage.

I've worked in almost every kind of dance. For four years, I did regional ballet, which is semi-professional work. I've also done the Broadway-musical style of dancing at dinner theaters and regional theaters. And I did modern dance for three years with small companies in Philadelphia and New York.

Anita leads guests at the spa in an aerobics class designed to increase their stamina.

One of the things I really enjoy about teaching is a class I've created, called "Dancing Through the Ages." It's a mix of dance styles dating back to the 1920s, including the Charleston, the jitterbug, the twist, disco, and funk. I also throw in several Broadway numbers. It's not the same as aerobics, but it's still a great workout. I have the students pretend they're wearing costumes and performing in front of an audience. People actually come to our spa just because of this class.

HOW I GOT STARTED:

As long ago as I can remember, I wanted to be a ballerina. My parents had friends who taught dance, and I started lessons when I was four and a half. I always wanted to be onstage. I took dance classes all through high school.

At 16, though, I gave up on ballet as a professional

Anita uses the bar to stretch her leg muscles before teaching a dance class at the spa.

pursuit, and in college I majored in physical education with a dance minor. Then I got a teaching job in Philadelphia, where I got the school to approve a dance major so that the kids could take my classes for credit, just like history.

While I was teaching, I started dancing again myself, and I realized that I had to go to New York to see whether I could make it as a professional dancer. There, I danced with a small modern company, got my first part in a musical, and went on to do various other work.

HOW I FEEL ABOUT IT:

It gives me great joy to see people react positively to an art form I truly love and to see the freedom they feel when they perform it themselves. Sometimes, dancing really changes their personalities. It's not simply good exercise, but something they really enjoy. People often ask me to come back with them and show their aerobics teachers at home how to do this. I see my work as sharing my love of dance with the public. And when I teach, I perform.

Still, there is nothing like performing on stage before a real audience. You bare your soul for them, which makes rejection hard to take. But dancers get rejected all the time. They compete with each other on a daily basis, and the competition isn't always subjective. If other dancers can raise their legs higher or point their toes better, they *are* better, and that's all there is to it. When you face that every day, it wears on you after a while.

WHAT YOU SHOULD KNOW:

Find a teacher who is encouraging and a studio in which you feel comfortable. Evaluate your strengths and weaknesses so that you can decide which type of dance to focus on. For Broadway musical dancing, they're hiring taller these days, so if you're a short dancer, you have to be aware of that and perhaps find other avenues.

If you major in dance in college, you're not qualified to do anything except dancing or teaching dance. So find something else you like and study that too, because a dancer's career is short. Lots of dancers retire at 30 or 35 and don't know what to do with themselves. They've never done or studied anything else. A theater degree is a possibility. Give yourself options.

A Broadway salary for a chorus dancer is about $700 a week. Most modern dance companies pay about the same. So, considering how short-lived this work is and the significant risk of injury, the money isn't great. You do it because you love it.

Anita has her students stretch before each class.

"At first I wasn't a great public speaker."

VINCE ERRICO

MARKETING EXECUTIVE

New York, New York

WHAT I DO:

I'm a marketing manager for a financial services company. Every company that sells a product has a marketing manager. The job of the marketing manager is to research the needs of the marketplace and then develop and market products to fill those needs. Here, we look at the marketplace to find out what financial services people want. Then we determine whether we can profitably provide those services.

For example, we recently made a decision, based on market research, to launch a new charge card. Part of my job involves briefing the advertising agency we're working with. We bring in their account team — which includes copywriters, artists, art directors, and experts in radio and television — and

Vince meets with copywriters from an advertising agency.

hold meetings to explain the product.

I also explain the product to the sales force. We have a national sales meeting once a year at which we conduct seminars and workshops. I have to present the product to hundreds of salespeople, which is very important. I have to make the product attractive and exciting to them so that they will believe in it and sell it to the public.

At first, leading the seminars wasn't much fun for me because I wasn't a great public speaker. But I made up for that by taking public speaking lessons. And I learned. I did six seminars back to back, and by the sixth one I was great. Meanwhile, I practiced a lot — practiced walking around the stage and doing the intonations. Some business executives even take acting lessons and go to speech experts to become more effective speakers.

Vince looks over the design for a new advertisement.

HOW I GOT STARTED:
I majored in German literature in college. After I graduated, I took some time off and traveled. Then I started working in a management training program at a savings and loan institution. Part of my job involved advertising and marketing, and the more I learned about the field, the more I enjoyed it. Finally, I realized that I enjoyed marketing more than banking. So, after five years at the savings and loan, I went back to business school.

HOW I FEEL ABOUT IT:
This work is constantly challenging, especially the launch of a new product. You have to push yourself to meet your deadlines and goals. You also have to push yourself to examine the potential payback over the coming years — that is, you need to determine whether the product will eventually become established and make money.

For me, the creative part is probably the most fun. It's like putting a puzzle together. You work with the ad agency to figure out the best way to describe your new product. The description has to be short, but it also has to make enough sense to grab the attention of the public.

WHAT YOU SHOULD KNOW:
You don't have to have an
M.B.A. to get into marketing,
but it's often hard to break in
without one. The argument
is that with a graduate business degree, you're already
fully trained in marketing,
operating theories, management, and so on. Many people
also believe that you should
study business as an undergraduate.

My thinking is different.
I think it's better to get a
broader education. My experience has been that people
with undergraduate degrees
in non-business areas seem
to do better because their
diverse experiences give
them a more useful per-
spective. For example, my
studies in German literature
improved my communication
skills, and that has definitely
helped me in this job. I have
to sell the sales force before
I can expect them to sell the
product, so I have to be
articulate. Public speaking
skills are important for any
business executive, but they
are especially critical for
someone in marketing working with a large sales force.

Pay for an entry-level posi-
tion varies depending on the
type of business and where
it's located. I'd say an average
starting salary for someone
with an M.B.A. is probably in
the $40,000 to $50,000
range. After five years or so,
your salary could be in the
$80,000 to $100,000 range.
And bonuses start to kick in
at that point, too.

Vince discusses a marketing plan with some colleagues.

"I can't just hide behind my desk."

KAREN CLAXTON
TEACHER
Berkeley, California

WHAT I DO:
I'm a computer teacher at a middle school. My primary responsibility is teaching a course to sixth graders introducing them to computers. Sometimes the software we use coordinates with other courses the students are taking in school. This way, the computers can be used as a tool for learning other subjects as well.

Because I teach a computer class, the students are usually quite motivated when they come into my classroom, so I can't just hide behind my desk. I have to move around a lot. I float from terminal to terminal, seeing how the kids are doing.

Besides the introductory course, I also teach elective classes to seventh and eighth graders. I can be creative with these electives, because

Karen helps students learn how to use a new software program.

the older students already know the basics. Now we can just have fun. For instance, we might create interesting designs using a computer graphics program. Then, using a heat-transfer ribbon, we can print out the designs and iron them onto T-shirts.

I have a fairly consistent work schedule. Each day has seven periods, and I teach during five of them — three introductory classes and two advanced electives. The rest of the time, I prepare lesson plans, correct papers, and eat lunch.

HOW I GOT STARTED:
I first thought I wanted to be a psychologist; then I thought I wanted to be a social worker. But once I took an education class in college, I knew I had found my calling.

I was very shy as a kid, and I never thought I'd be able to do this. It wasn't until that first education class that

Karen tries to make the lesson exciting for her students.

the concept of getting up in front of an audience really excited me.

I didn't really get interested in computers until I moved from New York to California and got a teaching job at a computer-oriented school. While teaching there, I learned how computers could be used to motivate students to learn. After that, I went to Berkeley and got a certificate in computers in education.

HOW I FEEL ABOUT IT:

I love teaching because of the satisfaction it brings, but also because I'm always onstage. When I first started out, I was self-conscious because of all the eyes staring at me. But you get used to it. There's

never a dull moment. I'm not just sitting at a desk — I'm performing.

WHAT YOU SHOULD KNOW:

If you're thinking about going into this work, you should enjoy helping people and communicating with them. As far as education goes, you need a four-year degree as a minimum, and I would recommend getting a master's degree, too.

Financially, teaching doesn't compare to many other professions. The starting salary in my district is $24,000 a year, and even after twenty-one years, the most you can make is $42,000. You can live on a teacher's income, but you won't get rich doing this.

Related Careers

Here are more performance-related careers you may want to explore:

AEROBICS INSTRUCTOR
Aerobics instructors lead group workouts at exercise studios and health clubs.

CIRCUIT LECTURER
Circuit lecturers travel around the country giving talks on their areas of expertise.

CLOWN
Clowns perform gags and stunts that make people laugh.

CRUISE DIRECTOR
Cruise directors organize and carry out all the social and recreational activities that take place aboard cruise ships.

DISC JOCKEY
Disc jockeys host music programs on the radio.

FLIGHT ATTENDANT
Flight attendants are responsible for the safety and comfort of passengers aboard an airplane.

MAGICIAN
Magicians perform tricks and optical illusions, such as pulling a rabbit out of a hat and sawing a person in half.

PRESS AGENT
Press agents represent celebrities and politicians in their interactions with the media.

PUBLIC ADDRESS ANNOUNCER
Public address announcers give the lineups and describe the events at sports arenas and ballparks.

SINGER
Singers perform in concerts and musicals as well as at recording sessions.

TOUR GUIDE
Tour guides lead groups of travelers all over the world. They explain the history and culture of the places they visit, organize excursions to local points of interest, and arrange for meals and accomodations.

WEATHERMAN
Weathermen predict the weather for television and radio shows.

Organizations

Contact these organizations for information
about the following careers:

TRIAL LAWYER
American College of Trial Lawyers
8001 Irvine Center Drive, #960, Irvine, CA 92718

DANCER
American Dance Guild
31 West 21st Street, New York, NY 10010

MUSICIAN
American Guild of Musical Artists
1727 Broadway, New York, NY 10019

TEACHER
American School Counselor Association
5999 Stevenson Avenue, Alexandria, VA 22304

NEWS ANCHORWOMAN
American Women in Radio and Television
1101 Connecticut Avenue, N.W., Suite 700, Washington, DC 20036

TALK SHOW HOST
National Association of Broadcasters
1771 N Street, N.W., Washington, DC 20036

MARKETING EXECUTIVE
National Council for Marketing and Public Relations
4322 16th Street, Greeley, CO 80634

COMEDIAN
Professional Comedians Association
581 Ninth Avenue, New York, NY 10022

PRESS AGENT
Public Relations Society of America
33 Irving Place, New York, NY 10003

JUGGLER
Ringling Brothers Clown College
1401 Ringling Drive South, Venice, FL 34285

ACTOR
Screen Actors Guild
7065 Hollywood Boulevard, Hollywood, CA 90028

STUNTMAN
Stuntmen's Association of Motion Pictures
4810 Whitsett Avenue, North Hollywood, CA 91607

Books

CAREERS AND MUSIC
Ed. by Malcolm E. Bessom and John T. Aquino. Reston, Va.:
Music Educators National Conference, 1977.

CAREERS AND OPPORTUNITIES IN MUSIC
By Alan Rich. New York: Dutton, 1964.

CAREERS AND OPPORTUNITIES IN TEACHING
By J.I. Biegelsen. New York: Dutton, 1969.

CAREERS AND OPPORTUNITIES IN THE THEATRE
By Jean Dalrymple. New York: Dutton, 1969.

CAREERS ENCYCLOPEDIA
Homewood, Ill.: Dow-Jones Irwin, 1980.

CAREERS IN COMMUNICATIONS
By Shonan Noronha. Lincolnwood, Ill.: VGM Career Horizons, 1987.

CAREERS IN EDUCATION
By Roy A. Edfeldt. Lincolnwood, Ill.: VGM Career Horizons, 1988.

CAREERS IN ELECTIVE GOVERNMENT
By Robert V. Doyle. New York: Julian Messner, 1976.

CAREERS IN MARKETING
By David W. Rosenthal. Englewood Cliffs, N.J.: Prentice Hall, 1984.

CAREERS IN THEATRE, MUSIC, AND DANCE
By Louise Horton. New York: Franklin Watts, 1976.

CAREERS WITH A CIRCUS
By Karin Kelly. Minneapolis, Minn.: Lerner Publications, 1975.

CREATIVE CAREERS
By Gary Blake and Robert W. Bly. New York: John Wiley, 1985.

MAKING IT IN THE MEDIA PROFESSIONS
By Leonard Mogel. Chester, Ct.: Globe Pequot Press, 1987.

VGM'S CAREERS ENCYCLOPEDIA
Lincolnwood, Ill.: VGM Career Horizons, 1988.

Glossary Index